A Bricklayer's Tales

Gary Troia

Gary Troia

Copyright 2013 by Gary Troia

All rights reserved. No part of this publication may be reproduced or transmitted in any form or by any mean,

electronic or mechanical, including photocopying, recording or any information storage system, without prior written consent from the author.
ISBN-13: 978-1489598714

DEDICATION

For Marina

CONTENTS

My Grandfather's Shed	Pg 1
What I Did in my Summer Holidays in 1000 Words	Pg 9
Angel Dust	Pg 17
Peyote	Pg 33
Return Ticket	Pg 43
The Day my Soul Left me	Pg 47
Advert in the Art Shop Window	Pg 53
Mrs. McClintock	Pg 81
The Unchangeable Chameleon	Pg 95
A Bricklayer's Tale	Pg 101

ALSO BY GARY TROIA

Spanish Yarns And Beyond

English Yarns And Beyond

The Complete Short Stories of Gary Troia

Ray Dennis Does *The Secret*

Coach to Como

Through the Porthole

ULOpia

MY GRANDFATHER'S SHED

My Grandfather's shed was shaped exactly like a child draws a house in England. He used to be a metalworker so there were many tools of that trade inside. I can't remember the names of the tools because I had no interest in metal, per se. I just remember the rasping file was used for smoothing out the rough edges.

My Grandfather used the shed to smoke his roll–ups. My Grandmother wouldn't let him smoke in the house even though she used to smoke herself, but quit. She said it wasn't good that my Brother and I breathed in the smoke when we visited, so he sat in the shed and smoked.

When the world became too unruly, I went and sat with my Grandfather in his shed.

We rarely spoke. I liked that. I think he did too, but I don't know for sure as I never asked him; I just felt at peace in the silence.
One summer day in a school holiday, he suddenly asked me if I would like to make something.
"Like what?" I said
"An adjustable spanner," he replied.
I thought about it for a little while..."ok."
I didn't know what an adjustable spanner was, so I thought about it for a while. I couldn't remember what a spanner looked like, never mind one that adjusted. As I was thinking, my Grandfather pulled out one of the heavy wooden draws from the bench and took out what I assumed was an adjustable spanner and placed it on the worktop.
I got up from the stool I was sitting on, and picked it up. I turned it around in my hands and started to twist the nut that moved the jaws. As I was moving the jaws one way and then the other, I looked at my Grandfather

and said:

"I don't think I'll be able to make this, Grandfather, it looks like quite a complex piece of engineering."

My grandfather burst out laughing. Then I did too.

"Why are you laughing", I said.

"You sounded like a young John Faraday," he said.

Then he started laughing again, as I started thinking: "Who is John Faraday?"

Then the door to my Grandfather's shed squeaked open. It was my Grandmother standing there with two steaming cups of tea and slices of Battenberg on a tray.

"Don't worry," he said, "you just watch and learn."

"Learn what? What are you two up to?" said Grandmother.

"We're going to make an adjustable spanner," I said.

"Well, to be honest, it's more of an English key than an adjustable spanner," said

Grandfather.

"Oh, right," said Grandmother, narrowing her eyes. "What's an English key?"

"It's like an adjustable spanner. John Faraday invented it," I replied.

"Did he now?" she said.

Grandfather was laughing again.

Then turning to my Grandfather, she said, "Make sure he doesn't hurt himself."

Grandfather nodded and rolled his eyes. Then Grandmother left, closing the squeaky shed door behind her.

Grandfather reached up to a shelf that held some old drawings of other things he had made. He pulled one out, put it on the worktop and blew some dust off. As he started to rummage around for a pencil, I considered the plate of Battenberg and saw there were three slices. Although I thought three slices for two people was a little strange, I was certain that Grandfather would let me eat two of them.

Grandfather started to draw with a pencil

and ruler as I began to eat the first slice of Battenberg. When the drawing was finished, he began to measure and cut pieces of metal. Then he took a discarded piece and put it in the vice, handed me the rasping file and told me to smooth out the rough edges.

After a couple of awkward attempts, he took the rasping file off me. He didn't say anything, just slowed by example. I watched intently as he showed me the way to do it. I soon got the hang of it, going back and forth and finding a rhythm that I instinctively knew was right. He tapped me on the shoulder for me to stop. Then he placed the first piece of the English key in the vice and told me to smooth it out to the line he had marked on it.

When he was satisfied that all the pieces were smoothed to the line, the process of drilling and riveting began. I watched with fascination as the English key emerged from nowhere.

By the time he finished and handed me the English Key, Grandmother had been back twice. The first time with cheese on toast, the second time with Belgian buns; and dusk had made an appearance as well.

I sat on the stool looking at the Completed English Key, then looked up at my Grandfather and said, "This was just an idea a few hours ago."

"Yes," he agreed, "everything is just an idea first."

I tried to think of a smart answer, but couldn't. I shivered instead.

In my bed that night, I went through what my Grandfather had said: "Everything is just an idea first." I looked around my bedroom and began listing other ideas: Bed, stereo, pyjamas, window, ball; was I an idea first? Each time I thought I had it; it broke apart and disintegrated just like the pictures in my kaleidoscope did when I turned it.

Years later, I thought of my Grandfather, the English key and what he had said about it. At first, the image was weak. But as I concentrated the image gradually tuned in; then through my Grandfather I perceived the smile of infinite intelligence satisfied with the extension of thought made manifest once again. Then again, it's probably just basic metalwork.

Gary Troia

WHAT I DID IN MY SUMMER HOLIDAYS IN 1000 WORDS

To be honest, me and the lads did exactly the same things as we do at any other time of the year. We would meet up in one of the old shelters in the grounds of the abandoned Arsenal and drink and take drugs. Occasionally there would be the odd outbreak of random violence, but nothing too heavy.

Once we had all conglomerated at the shed, we would pool our money together that everyone had managed to lay their hands upon, then we would decide what amount and type of drugs we could get for the day. To be honest, it usually just consisted of hash, alcohol and speed.

When we had decided upon the order (usually after much debate), me and Col would make our way to Blow John's to buy it. It was always me and Col as we were the only two of the group he would allow in his house. Blow John and his house fascinated me as it reminded me of the sweetshop at the top of my road – it seemed to have everything, and you could pick and mix. Heroin, coke, speed, leb, red leb and oil were just some of the products on offer.

No matter what time we seemed to go to Blow John's, the music was always blaring out from his massive speakers. We would have to wait for at least ten minutes before Blow John would answer the door because he could not hear us. Furthermore, we were on strict instructions to tap on the front window lightly, so we tried to coincide the tapping at the end of each track – a fucking nightmare if he was playing Pink Floyd.

Once inside, me and Col knew that time was

not of the essence, owing to Blow John being heavily smacked up and wanting to talk to us about music. I didn't care, Blow John fascinated me.

When me and Col were seated on the settee that had no innards to it (our arses were literally on the floor), Blow John began the long process of sorting himself out some smack on silver foil. Once he had had his go, he would offer it to me and Col, but we always turned him down. Then he would praise us for turning it down.

Back at the shelter, after the initial frenzied drug taking had petered out, the action and conversation became a reflection of the hot summer's day; languid, dopey, and very long.

I was rocking about in a rickety wooden chair smoking a joint, looking through the broken skylight at the pale blue sky, and thinking about going back to school a week and a half later. Then I randomly mentioned that it would be a result if someone burnt the school down so we didn't have to go back in a week and a half.

Sometimes you just never know that when you say something, anything, people can just latch on to it. This is how it transpired with my throw away remark about someone burning down the school. By the end of the day the remark had changed from "I hope someone would burn down the bloody school" to "we can do this thing." In addition, Jazz and Micky Boy began having a row about whose idea it was first. I just kept quiet; waiting to see how the scenario would play itself out.

By the end of the week, the scenario had turned into a plan. So much so that the fund for alcohol and drugs took a secondary position, owing to a more important fund for items such as cloths, petrol and balaclavas.

Three days later two petrol cans were sitting menacingly in the old shelter. The next stage was to find the heroes that were going to carry out the attack. There was much argument and debate. It seemed that everyone was up for it. Finally, Jazz, Donnie, Trev and Johnny won the day. I made out the decision not to include me was poor, but I didn't push my dismay or fight too hard to have the decision overturned. Micky Boy, who many considered to be the hardest in the school – although to be honest I had my doubts - was now claiming sole ownership of the idea.

At 9pm, four days before we were due back in school, me and Micky Boy took the lift to the eighteenth floor of the tower block that overlooked our place of learning and waited for the imminent arson attack that was about to be launched upon it.

About an hour later, Micky Boy shouted, "Look" and pointed to four bent over figures running across the lawn by the sixth form block. Then we lost sight of them as they disappeared behind some bushes and trees.

"Well, Micky Boy," I said, "looks like your plan is about to be implemented."

The look he gave me only strengthened my view of him not being the hardest in the school.

Nothing at all seemed to happen for the next few minutes. Then I saw a faint glow inside the sixth form block. Then there was another. Suddenly, without any expectation of what was going to occur next, I saw a sizable conflagration erupt. I could easily visualize the books, tables and paper burning inside the sixth form block.

The rest, as they say, is history. Jazz, Donnie, Trev and Johnny are now in borstal. Micky Boy is still dining out on the idea, and the sixth form block is undergoing refurbishment.

I have learned much from this particular summer holiday, but above all I have realised that ideas can catch fire just as quick as a sixth form block can.

PS. Miss Stanton could you let me know in

your notes if having ideas might ever be considered a criminal act?

Absolvi meam animam.

Gary Troia

ANGEL DUST

I was laying bricks in a Maryland suburb. Only my third week in the USA and things were changing on a daily basis at a rapid rate. I'd met Melanie in a bar in London. She was on holiday with her friends and I was out and about with mine. We got talking and for the rest of her holiday I was a tour guide for her. She liked the tour so much that she started to write to me regularly, eventually inviting me out to Maryland where she lived.

So I got my head down and saved money. I told family and friends that I would be back in about a month as I assumed my money would run out by then.

On landing at Baltimore Washington International airport, I was met by Melanie and a lovely looking Latina called Virginia, who I took an instant liking to. Unfortunately, two days later, Virginia had to travel to Los Angeles for her grandmother's funeral. I spent my days reading books in the yard and listening to the racket the crickets made. I thought of Virginia a fair bit for the first couple of days then put her out of my mind as it was unlikely that I would see her again. I was wrong. Two days later Melanie received a postcard from Los Angeles. Part of it asked if I was having a good time. She was thinking about me too. Two days later, she returned.

Melanie used to call me from work once a day. One day I asked her to phone Virginia to see if she fancied going out for the day. We drove out into the countryside. We saw each other every day after that to the point where she asked me to move in with her at her mum's house. So I did, much to the annoyance of Melanie, who I never saw again.

When Virginia went to work, I thought about having to go back to England. This thought filled me with dread and disappointment as I was in my element. I even phoned the immigration department and asked if I could get a work permit. Of course, I couldn't. Regardless, I decided to look in the local paper for work. The advertisements: I looked under B for bricklayers and was vexed to find that there weren't any. I continued to read the ads and cheered right up when I reached M. Americans call bricklayers masons and there were at least thirty. There was a building boom going on. I looked through them and chose one at random. I phoned and explained who I was and what I could do. He seemed very pleased and mentioned that the foreman was from Liverpool and would sure like to have another limey on the team. I put the phone down and immediately thought that I should have told them I'd start in a couple of days' time to get my head around it.

We went to the hardware store when she got in to buy the tools of the trade. I slept fitfully through the night, worrying about the work.

 The following morning Virginia dropped me off at the site and handed me my packed lunch. I worked well that day. Everyone was impressed. At the end of it, Colin, the Scouse foreman came towards me looking sullen. He said that as this was a government job, they would not be able to pay me "under the table," as he put it, and would be sorry to see me go. I thanked him anyhow. He gave me cash for my day's work. I was dispirited. We both were. The weekend was a drag.

On Monday morning when Virginia had gone to work, I made myself a coffee and had another look at the paper. I mulled it over and assumed that all the contractors must have the same policy, but something kept nagging at my mind, telling me to give it another go. I turned to the page of masons again, and indiscriminately dropped my finger on one. The guy I spoke to said he was very pleased I'd called. There was definitely a boom going on and the building firms were having a hard time getting enough masons. He agreed to me starting and told me where the site was. I told him I didn't have a green card. He told me not to worry, as they would work it out. The problem was, I told him, when calling him back after consulting with Virginia that the site was too far away and we only had one car between us. He rang me back saying he'd arranged for one of the other masons to pick me up and drop me back as he lived just down the street from me.

Everything was in place and it all pointed to being a great start. The only problem was that Vinnie the lift was a raving drug addict and alcoholic. Every night on the way home, we had to stop at a liquor store and buy a six-pack of beer, which he set on his lap and drained, one after another. I was also regaled with some of his fantasies of what he could have been given the right circumstances.

One evening he started to slap wildly on the steering wheel with his hands.

"Should have been a drummer," he said. "See what I did there?"

I tried to think what he had done there, if I had missed something; something other than him just slapping his hands like a maniac on the steering wheel whilst driving along the freeway. I didn't want to upset him. For one he was very volatile, and two he was my lift to work.

"Err, not sure," I said, unwisely asking him to do it again.

He quite happily did it again; then waited for an answer. I didn't have a clue.

"You limeys have got some good music, but you don't seem to know shit about it," he said.

He did the thing with his hands on the steering wheel again and said, "Fucking paradiddles, man!"

The rest of the journey was spent with him going on about how he should have been in a rock band, and going on and on that I should get into Lynard Skynard. The following evening after work, he stopped for his usual six-pack. Then he said that we were going to make a detour as he had run out of Phenylcyclohexyl-Piperdine, colloquially known as Angel Dust.

I was reasonably up on illegal drugs, having taken the majority of the ones on offer in England. I'd heard all sorts of stories about Angel Dust being one of the most dangerous drugs on the planet – two stories in particular. An old woman hurled a police officer through a plate glass window, and an up and coming rapper who had gouged one of his eyes out and is now in a mental hospital; but they may be urban myths, I don't know.

We pulled off the freeway and made our way on a different route that was unknown to me. As we drove on, I began to feel a little uneasy at what I was seeing. No longer the suburban houses of Maryland as I was used to. It started to get very built up with what I would call, in England, rough looking housing estates. We pulled over on a street with tenements either side.

It was dusk as we pulled over and the yellowy–orange streetlights contributed to the drama of the situation I was in. The effect of our car in the neighborhood caused mass movement within it. Those that were seated stood up, and those already up began moving like a colony of disturbed bats swooping towards our car. The colony was all about us now. I noticed that the door latch was up on my side. I nonchalantly rested my forearm on the latch, locking it. Seconds later, there were four, then more and more dangerous looking guys converging on both sides of the car. Vinnie had his window down and was doing deals. But every time he struck a deal with one of them, another muscled his way in offering a better one. At last, a package was thrust through the window as he passed dollars in the other direction. Vinnie sat staring at the package, I muttered under my breath for him to drive on. Then, a hand, as quick as you like, came through the window in a blur and snatched some dollars from the top pocket of his jacket.

"Fucking drive!" I said.

He took my advice and drove out of there.

"Fucking hell!" was all I could think to say after that.

Soon we were pulling over in a country lane. He opened a beer and gulped it down before making two joints. Angel dust comes in different forms: pills, liquid or sprayed directly onto marijuana. This was the latter version. When he finished rolling, he put one in his mouth and lit it. The other he gave to me. I put mine in my jacket pocket and said I would smoke it later.

Driving along the freeway, I detected a change in him without looking. When I turned to my left, he was sitting way back in his chair with his arms straight out holding the steering wheel as if major G–force was having an effect on him. I wasn't far wrong as he suddenly exclaimed that he should have been an F-1-11 pilot. I was tense and on edge by the time we pulled over at Virginia's - probably landing in his warped mind. Virginia managed a restaurant in the evening, and by the time I got in from my adventure we only had twenty minutes together before she left for work.

I took a shower, went down stairs, cracked upon a cold beer and settled down listening to some music. I couldn't relax. All the time I could hear the joint in my jacket pocket calling me.

"Smoke me," I heard it call..."smoke me... you know you want me...smoke me..."

I tried to ignore it, but before long, I was up there standing in the bedroom, with it in one hand, a lighter in the other, and looking at myself in a full-length mirror. I knew it was wrong. I knew it was dangerous. I also knew I was going to smoke it.

Soon I felt the effects of the marijuana sweeping gently through me. It was strong, very strong. I went back down stairs to get another beer – maybe it wasn't going to be so bad after all.

Then it hit me, wave after wave of strong drugs pounding through my mind and body. It wouldn't relent. I started to panic. I felt my heart racing. I saw my heart thum-ping thum-ping through my shirt. I drank more beer to help. It didn't, so I panicked some more. I became even more panicked when I remembered I was in the USA.

I went upstairs, had a shower, and came down again. Then I went back up to have another shower - I thought I could just wash the nasty drug away.

I sat down at the thick wooden table in the kitchen and thought to myself that if I put my arms under both ends of the table, I would be able to lift them up and snap it in two. I then thought about the rapper who had gouged his eye out, which didn't help. I said to myself, over and over: "No matter what happens, don't gouge your fucking eyes out, whatever you do."

Then I had an epiphany in a space between the drug and me. I know what is going on here, I thought. I'm being dissociated by the drug. I'm oscillating between sanity and insanity. I wondered if I could hold on to the sanity (albeit stoned sanity). At least then I would understand that when the mania begun again, I would be able to ride out the storm. The other idea was to stand back in being, and watch sanity and insanity act the scene out in front of me like a play.

I then had the idea of reading a book. I found Peter Wright's Spycatcher, positioned myself in a wicker chair in the bedroom, crossed my legs a la professorial, furrowed my brow and concentrated. This seemed to be doing the trick. I will read until the drug has had its way with me. The more I ignore it, the quicker it will get bored and leave me alone.

Things were going splendidly until I became aware of reading aloud in Greek. I don't speak Greek! But it seemed so clear and plausible. I put the book down and looked at myself in the mirror. I saw myself in an ancient Greek symposium and assumed I was speaking to Plato, Aristotle and other learned Greeks on philosophy. Then again, they could have been Romans, and maybe it was Pliny the Elder and his mates I was discoursing with. Either way, I didn't want to disappoint them, so I really put my heart and soul into it. I was up, strolling around the bedroom, pausing occasionally for the right sentiment. The ancients were lapping it up, enraptured at my new way of thinking. They even started asking me questions. I would give a brilliant answer to which they applauded with respect for my insight. At other times I would respond with a witty response that had them rolling around laughing.

As I reveled in my genius, I began to sense liquid all over my body. I also sensed my head heating up and I began panting like a large dog. I looked in the mirror and had a major shock. I seemed to be melting like an action man in a fire.

I could no longer take the heat, so I removed my sweat-soaked t–shirt and jeans, then began parading around in just my pants. When I had the courage to look in the mirror again, I was no longer a melting man, but a nubile, muscular warrior. I started to shadow box, kick out and head butt the opponent in the mirror who gave as good as he got. I gave in first. My punches and kicks no longer had any determination in them.

I spent the rest of the night walking from

room to room, being unable to settle, lying down, rolling around moaning. Then I saw the light from Virginia's headlights shining through the window. I raced downstairs, sat in one of the armchairs trying my best to look as normal as I could with my legs crossed and my arms folded. She took one look at me before saying: "you've smoked that joint, haven't you; and why are you sitting in just your pants?"

"I'm overheating," I said, before collapsing to my knees and hugging her thighs.

"Please help me!"

Gary Troia

PEYOTE

Last week I had a couple of jobs, delivering drugs to dealers and laying glass blocks in Santa Monica. Last night a friend who is a hippy introduced me to a group of hippies. Today I'm waiting for those hippies to pick me up to spend a few days with them on a remote ranch in Arizona to take what Brother Bill Hicks used to describe as an "heroic dose" of peyote.

The VW camper van pulled up, the door slid open and I got in. I took my position and off we went to Arizona with a huge joint of grass that went from one to the other around the van. When the joint was at the front of the van, the wind caught it and burning ember came off it and hit me just below my right eye. I felt like saying,

"Fucking hell, hippy, be careful," but thought it was not appropriate to start the trip in that manner. The irritation below my eye bothered me for the rest of the day. I spent the rest of journey stoned, looking out the window.

It was early evening when we arrived at the ranch; it was definitely remote. Built of brick and wood on just one floor, it looked very peaceful. Inside the furniture was old but very tasteful with Indian style rugs on the polished wood floor.

We all agreed that we would take it easy that night, just a couple of beers and a few joints. That is how we spent the night.

After breakfast, we all converged in the main living room. Mike, who had introduced me to the hippies, spoke a bit about peyote and singled me out in his little talk. I told him that I had taken LSD before, but he continued explaining to me that this was unadulterated peyote juice and very strong and just wanted me to be aware of that.

Mick then asked us all to sit in a circle in to become as one for the upcoming experience. Once the seated circle formed, Melissa, I think her name was, went to the kitchen and brought in a small bottle that had a very dark liquid inside. Then, with the aid of a pipette, she went around the group administering the drug by way of three little drops on the tongue. Then we held hands and sat in the circle for far too long.

I began generating too much heat, so I asked if I could take a lovely old rocking chair outside for a bit of air. I began gently rocking back and forth, taking large intakes of air and puffing them out noisily. I then felt quite queasy, so I stopped rocking. I felt I was going to vomit. Mick emerged on the veranda and I started to ask him if the way I felt was normal. He assured me that the nausea would soon fade away.

"And the heat?"

"Yeah, that too, it will all simmer down in a

few minutes."

I should have listened to what Mick had to say in the circle.

I didn't know whether to rock, sit still, stand up or lay down.

Mick brought me a glass of water. I gulped it down.

Gradually everyone came out to sit on the veranda. I looked at the others and they all seemed to be handling the experience much better than me. A couple of the hippies brought out a table. Upon it they placed jugs of iced water, homemade lemonade and a big bowl of fruit. Before I knew it, my body temperature had cooled and I was no longer feeling nauseous. I was just staring at the fruit. There was a pineapple, watermelon, oranges and apples. The fruit delighted me, especially the cut segments of watermelon. The pink-red flesh with the black seeds was the most incredible thing I had ever seen. I knew that only God could have thought and created such a thing. I contemplated if I were God would I have thought of such a thing? No, not really, was my instant conclusion. At an almighty push, I assumed I might have created water and probably the potato.

The LSD I had taken before was a veritable toddler to the mature adult power of peyote. Everything seemed so marvelous and had so much hidden depth to it; I just didn't have the vocabulary to explain what I was seeing to myself; holy, holy, holy.

I was rocking and staring out at the landscape when Mick came and asked me if I wanted to go to town for provisions and a bite to eat. I was so at peace that I felt the town might miss out if I didn't go, so four of us made our way to town in the VW camper van.

I don't know if it was the motion of the VW, but I started to feel light headed and warm again, breathing in and out to regain the feeling I had just lost. Mick asked me if I was all right with a grin on his face. Then the van erupted with laughter.

"What?" I asked

"You are huffing and puffing really loudly," said Mick.

Paranoia crept in and I wished I had stayed back at the ranch. By the time we reached the town and parked, I felt like staying in the van until they came back, but I thought better of it as I didn't want to be alone.

Let's go and eat first and check out the experience and get the provisions later was the plan. We found a diner that was very dark inside. I got squashed up to the wall and felt claustrophobic. I was almost on the verge of freaking out and not being able to control myself. The others were looking at the menus and interacting well, but I felt like an alien at the party. Looking at the menu seemed too difficult a task; it was if I had never heard of the items on the menu. Not only that, but the idea of eating food was almost anathema to me, so I played safe and ordered a Coke.

When the food arrived, it almost made me sick. Fortunately, it was all salad stuff as the hippies were vegetarian, but I could smell the meat from other tables and it was excruciatingly off-putting to my sensibilities. However, once my Coke arrived, sipping it took me back to my original feeling of wonder I had experienced with the watermelon. It was just so sweet and perfect. The coldness and effervescence was something else that I had never truly comprehended before.

Calmness had returned to me and soon I joined in the banter and felt so much more at ease. Mick said that it was time for us to get the provisions. A sudden outflow of generosity came over me as I said that I would pay the bill. The hippies seemed impressed by that.

Back at the ranch, all was set for our next excursion to a lake. I was still tripping, but it was far more controllable and comfortable. The lake was an idyllic refuge from the hustle and bustle of the town and I lapped it up.

The shimmer on the water fascinated me. I used to think that a shimmer was just an aspect on the water caused by the sun, but no, it was its own entity just like the water and the sun.

Those few hours spent at the lake remain some of my best investments ever.

Back at work on Monday morning, standing on the scaffold, I tried to keep the vision alive, thought hard to keep the faith, but it was nigh on impossible.

A Bricklayer's Tales

Gary Troia

RETURN TICKET

There is always a first time for everything. This is the first time I've waited to board a plane handcuffed to a sheriff. I don't know if he is an actual sheriff – he may be a deputy for all I know - but he does have one of those metal star-like badges you see in westerns, I just can't get a proper look at it as the handcuffs prohibit my movement.

I'm sitting in the departure lounge at Baltimore Washington International Airport, and all the adults in the lounge are pretending not to look at the sheriff and me. Their children, however, are still unhampered by social protocol. The parents continually yank their children back from trying to find out what they themselves are dying to know. I feel like shouting out, "It was only a bit of hash, for fuck's sake, I'm quite sure you've all had a crafty one?"

Me and the sheriff are last off the bus. We wait whilst everyone boards the plane. The sheriff hands my passport to the chief purser, unfastens the handcuffs, and then I too board the plane. In my seat I take one last perfunctory look at the land of the free, then slam the plastic shutter down on three years of my life.

There was always a room for me at my Gran's house, and after giving her a necessary but unlikely story, I went to my room to lie down. I tried hard to prevent the recent trauma from overwhelming me, but it was hard, too hard. My Grandparents decorated this room for me when I was a child, the wallpaper depicted cowboys and Indians, and all I could think was that the cowboys have triumphed again.

A Bricklayer's Tales

Gary Troia

THE DAY MY SOUL LEFT ME

"But be holy in the presence of God, or you will not know that you are there." A Course in miracles.

Staggering, stumbling, tripping for years, here it comes now the fall. Through the letterbox of my new apartment fell the letter that confirmed my dismissal from the college where I worked at teaching brickwork, the final confirmation of terrible causes. On building sites, the manhandling of another person does not carry such a hefty penalty as it does at a college.
Pursuing a policy of burning bridge after bridge finally brings you to a place where the land around you is completely charred, where nothing is living, and there is nothing

left to burn. Each moment seems to take an eternity to pass, and hope is just four randomly assembled letters in a dictionary.

My apartment, like the contacts in my phone, was unfurnished. There was nothing to do but walk for miles and miles. When I returned with wine, there was nothing to do but drink for relief.

Through the silence, I heard the front door of my apartment being manipulated. I was startled like a deer. I listened like a bat. Maybe I was hearing things? I wasn't. The sounds continued. I walked stealthily to the kitchen and fetched a carving knife, all the while the sounds continued. I was now standing at the front door. A sheet of plastic was protruding through. Someone was trying to unlock the latch. I was aware that the intruder was close to opening the door, yet I was unafraid because I was numb to the world. The chain was on, so it was impossible for them to open the door fully. It was them because I heard them whispering to one another. I crouched down and put my ear to the door; I was about to do something. They were still whispering to each other when I whispered to them, "I'm just going to remove the catch, then I will stab you."

The sheet of plastic withdrew as quickly as a snake's tongue. They were now silent. They were unsure of what they heard, if anything at all. Long seconds passed before the sheet of plastic returned. Again they began to manipulate the door. I was still crouching with the carving knife in my hand. I whispered almost imperceptibly, "I'm just going to release the chain from the door." Then, with a quick yank, I released the chain and flung open the door. The look of horror in their eyes was magnificent as they saw me no longer crouching, but reared up with the carving knife in my hand. They screamed as I chased them down the fire escape, but they were too fast for me.

The potential burglary and subsequent

chase had the effect of a defibrillator on my heart, but my mind remained immune to it.

Through years of debilitating depression, my most loyal of all companions were alcohol and drugs, they just took the edge off, or, in the words of a former friend, "took the dairy off the day." Now I was going to ask them for one last favour. I took the bottle of sleeping pills my Doctor prescribed and put it in my pocket. Then I put a bottle of vodka in my fashionable, soft leather brief case and walked to a little wooded area just behind the local golf course. And it was there I began my personal picnic. I no longer had any concerns about the rights and wrongs of my decision as my soul had also had enough and was absent without leave, leaving behind it just another empty shell on a beach. Through the gaps in the trees I occasionally glimpsed golfers putting...but soon I was very, very sleepy.

It took me a few minutes on waking before I

realised what had occurred. Then deep sadness gripped me so tightly it was almost too bittersweet for words. I knew immediately that my soul would never leave me. It was me all along that refused to hear the gentle voice that went unheard because of my perception of an empty shell; for there is no empty shell in the world, when put to an ear, but lacks the faint echo of the sea.

Gary Troia

ADVERT IN THE ART SHOP WINDOW

I was between jobs again. The majority of my working life has been spent between jobs. I'd just finished building the walls of a small swimming pool at a house in Tunbridge Wells. My pocket was cash rich, but it wouldn't last long. I would use it to allow me a space to be able to live, think and drink until it ran out. Then I'd have to find another building job. And so my world would continue to turn. I detested building work, but I knew of nothing else where I could earn decent enough money to take regular breaks from the grind. I had a drink.

The following morning I went for a walk around town. The weather was cold and trying to rain. My hangover reminded me constantly that only more drinking would alleviate it. Soon I came to an art shop. I stopped there and looked through the window. I noticed a section with postcards in the window advertising this thing and that service. As I perused the cards without too much interest, one suddenly caught my eye. It said: "Wanted, looking for a building manager to run a renovation of a house in a small village in Andalusia. Estimated three months work. Call the number below if interested." I whipped out my phone, tapped in the number, saved it, and walked on. I went to Sainsbury's and bought my groceries and wine for the weekend, then plotted up in a pub and settled down for a couple of hours.

I took out my phone and had a look at the Spanish number I had just entered into my phone. I thought that getting the job would be a good idea. Then I decided I had neither the energy to see the job out, nor the inclination to move to Spain. So I put it in my pocket, picked up my pint and supped it. When a couple of pints had overcome my edgy hangover, I soon felt that of course I would have the energy to run the job, and moving to Spain would be a good idea. I'd also be out of the cold and the sunshine would do me good. So I began to list my credentials to myself: I know a fair bit about building. I also have a degree in Spanish — how many builders could boast that when applying for the job? So buoyed by my lager confidence I rang the number. There was no answer, so I left a message and forgot all about it.

I was sat staring at a packet of Butterscotch Angel Delight in one of the Sainsbury's bags when the phone rang. It was from the company I'd just built the swimming pool for. They wanted to know if I was up for cleaning some brickwork using brick cleaning acid. I told them I was going on holiday for a while. I was almost certain that I would get the Spanish job, and so it turned out, as a couple of pints later the phone rang again. It was the Spanish number so I put my professional hat on. The upshot of the conversation, which was unusually brief, was that I should get a flight as soon as possible. And after booking it I was to let him know so he could arrange to pick me up at the airport. When I asked him how I would recognize him, he replied that he looked like Mick Jagger. I told him that I was between jobs and it wouldn't be long before I would arrive. Four or five days I told him. He said that that would be fine as long as it was no more than that. I assured him it wouldn't be any longer than that. He also said that he would reimburse the flight money and I would be able to stay in the house that was being done up as the majority of the work that needed to be done was external.

So with that, I had received the best news for a long time. Things were changing for the better and I would have a massive adventure into the bargain. I started to feel like someone who mattered. I was getting a flight to my job and that seemed very important to me. I immediately vowed to get myself together in the next few days. I would stop drinking, eat well, and practice my Spanish as I was obviously going to have to order materials and the work force were bound to be Spanish.

I rubbed my hands, sank into the hefty arm chair in the front room, turned on the gas fire, lit a cigarette and unscrewed a cork from a bottle of Rioja. None of the furniture was mine. I had very few clothes. My only possessions that meant anything to me were my books, which I had somehow managed to keep hold of despite my constant moving from one place to another. I called my mate C who had agreed to look after them. I hired a man and a van and took them to C's house in Catford. So all was sorted and I could fly out immediately if I wanted to. I had already decided that it would be best to prepare myself for a few days. I would just leave and not tell the landlord. I would lose my deposit, but it was worth it. I looked around the one bed flat and realised just how depressing it was. I must have somehow put it out of my mind knowing I had to live there, but now its true ugliness reared up a at me.

Once I had placed my books in safe care and ordered my easyJet flight, sitting and waiting in that flat become so depressing that I just had to have a drink. I then vowed that when I arrived in Spain I would stop thinking and drinking and make the most of the amazing opportunity and become the man that my potential has always alluded to. I had been given so many opportunities in my life that I had just frittered away - and who knows if God only gives each person a certain amount? Fuck! My flight to Spain was early in the morning. I decided that I would get a cab to the airport the night before. I could then enjoy pretending to be someone important and have a drink at the bar. I bought myself a bottle of vodka and a container of orange juice and emptied them both in to an empty Evian bottle. I had drunk a fair bit of the vodka before the cab arrived as I couldn't fit it all in. I was literally in good spirits as I bantered with the cab driver all the way to Gatwick. I checked in, went to the bar, and got talking with one passenger after another until they all literally departed one after another. After a time I got tired so I went and sat on the benches. I started to read my book and swigged the vodka and orange from the water bottle. The drink took hold and soon I had to lie down. I was woken up by armed police demanding to see my passport.

As the 5am flight grew nearer, I sat myself up feeling the blood in my head whooshing around, making me feel befuddled. I knew immediately that I had reached the stage of drunk where it was going to be nigh on impossible to hide it. This was not good, as I had still to navigate the boarding part of the airport experience. I began deep breathing exercises, but it didn't help. I remonstrated with myself for being so stupid, but that didn't help. I really only ever drank beer and wine which I knew how to harmonize properly the majority of the time. Why I chose to drink spirits before my new opportunity, God only knows. Then I heard the call for passengers for the easyJet flight to Malaga. I breathed deeply, looked down at my bag and slumped back in my seat. The first thought was to forget about the flight, just go home and explain to Mick Jagger that I was feeling a bit rough, and I would fly out as soon as I felt better. Then I envisioned myself in bed at home, drinking wine and beating myself up at missing the golden opportunity that I had yearned so long for.

No, I must crack on, I can manage it. I began to make my way to the called gate number. I knew that I was staggering, but I just couldn't gain control of my walking, no matter how hard I tried. I called upon my entire inner being to help counteract the stagger, but it was too little, too late. I might get a couple of steps going in a forward motion, but when I thought I had it, to the left or the right I would lurch once again.

I soon viewed the gate and saw that a few people were already in line, handing over there tickets and passports. I sat in a chair and made sure I had all my documents at hand so as not to fumble around in my bag when it was my turn. Although I was very drunk, I was also very nervous, which is one of the worst drunken states to be in. I had an idea that I should stand in line and shuffle along as the queue moved forward. As I was standing in line and looking out at the plane I was hopefully going to be sitting on, I received a tap on the arm and a request to follow the man who had just tapped it. I followed him away from the other passengers. Then he said the dreaded words: "We think you are too drunk to board, sir." With my last bit of sensible thinking I could muster, I said: "Yes, sir, I am very drunk, but I have an unnatural fear of flying, and although drunk, I am a quiet drunk and just wanted to make sure I slept through the flight." With that he asked for my documents and said, "Follow me."

To my surprise, he led me passed the woman who was taking the tickets and on to the plane. I followed him down the aisle to the rear of the plane. Once I had taken my seat, he tapped me on the shoulder and said: "you have a good sleep." I thanked him. I woke and opened and shut my eyes a number of times as everything was very blurry. I couldn't believe my fortune. We had landed and I couldn't remember a thing about the flight. As my focus began to gain more clarity, I worked out that I was still in London! Fuck! Not only did I sleep through the flight to Malaga, I've slept through the return flight to London. I got up, turned to the two stewards standing by the toilets, and said, "I must have forgotten to get off in Malaga." The guy who got me on the plane, took me back to my seat and said, "We haven't taken off yet!" I remember nothing until I woke again as the plane was about to land at Malaga.

As I reached up to get my bag from the locker, I caught the eye of the steward, my mate. I nodded my head in gratitude to him. He returned the nod that simultaneously said, you are welcome, now fuck off. My hangover was extreme and I felt grimy. So after gaining access to Spanish territory, I made my way to the toilets and looked in the mirror. I looked rough, but that was understandable. So I whipped off my shirt and doused myself with water and soap in the hope of making myself presentable. I did the pits first, then the face, and finished by damping my hands with water and running them through my hair. People came and went while I was in the toilets – I was half expecting them to alert the authorities to a man in the toilets with no top on, but they didn't. I threw my shoulders back, breathed in a massive hit of oxygen and emerged on to the concourse feeling and looking all the better for it.

There were many people waiting for passengers from our flight, so I held back, waiting for relatives and friends to be reunited and thinning the crowd in the process so that I would be able to spot Mick Jagger easier. Even so, no matter how hard I scanned, I still could not locate a wiry individual with a battered face. Then we made eye contact. Some of the description sat true as he approached me. He certainly had a well lived-in visage, but with a drinker's bulbous nose. The blood vessels in it had burst some time ago. He wasn't a svelte like creature, either. He had a fair old beer gut, and looked unkempt, which made me feel so much better about myself.

As we got talking in his Volvo, with me outwardly trying to look and sound like the kind of man who would be able to run his job, while inside my whole body and every cell was screaming out for a drink. I was hoping that he didn't expect me to start today, I thought, as there was no chance I would be able to handle it. It was Friday, so there was a good chance that I would be able to recover by Sunday night. Then he said, almost immediately after my thought, "We obviously won't be starting today, so we'll stop at a restaurant on the way for a drink and a bite to eat."

It was still relatively early, and now I was thinking about how I could get a drink in without looking like a gasping alcoholic. We pulled up at the restaurant, found a table and he asked what I wanted. "You know what?" I said, "I might just unwind a bit with a caña." He motioned to the waiter and asked for a caña and a whisky. The old bulbous nose wasn't lying. Here was an alcoholic of the first order. He was already growing on me. I began to feel recharged again. The beer was placed in front of me. The medicine was there, but I felt a little bit of the shakes and was horrified to think that my hand might shake as I picked up the glass. Fortunately, as I was thinking long and hard about getting the medicine into my system, he said, "Fancy something to eat? They do some tasty sardines here."

"Okay," I said. Then as he went to order them, I downed around two-thirds of the beer. I got up to go to the toilet, and on the way back, noticing he was back at the table, I ordered another round of drinks. As we were eating, drinking became easier, and down they went, oiling the machine. I was beginning to feel so much better as the alcohol weaved its magic potion.

After a few more drinks, we drove to the very small village where he lived. It was literally in the middle of nowhere. "There are only twelve houses in the village, and I own two of them," he said. "You will be living in the one that needs completing, but don't worry, the majority of the work is external, and it's more than habitable. He was right. The house wasn't bad at all. He asked if I fancied coming up to his house after I'd had a sleep. He said that he would make dinner. Things were looking up. I had a look around the house and decided that there was nothing too complicated for me to worry about. I was feeling very pleased with the way things were going. He said that he would invite a couple of others from the village, too.

"Oh," he said, turning around, there are a few beers in the fridge, so help yourself to them."

I opened the fridge and took out a lovely cold San Miguel. As I sat on the sofa, surrounded by tools that were all over the place, I noticed there were also some bottles of red wine. So I opened one of them. I was feeling so relaxed. When I woke up, I had no idea of the time, but by the look of the dark sky I was going to be late for dinner. I was two hours late after checking my phone. I quickly splashed my face with water, sprayed on some after-shave and headed up the steep path to his house. There were huge iron gates. I rang the bell, but there was no answer. I rang it again. I must have stood there for half an hour before deciding to go back to the house. I opened another bottle of red wine. When I woke the following morning, I noticed a note that had been pushed under the door. It read: The last guy let me down. You have let me down. I cooked a good meal for you, and you couldn't be bothered to show. So it's not going to work out."

"Fucking hell," I thought, "I've only been here one night, and I've already been sacked."

So I opened up another bottle of red wine to help me decide what I should do. I tried on no fewer than five occasions to ring his bell that day and try to talk about it with him, but he never answered.

The following day happened to be the village feria, which I went to as there was nothing else to do. Might as well enjoy myself, I thought. There was a trio of girls in a band. A massive paella was being cooked, which was handy, I was starving. By this time I couldn't care less if I ever got to see Mick Jagger again. I got talking with others who lived in the village. I told them what had happened and they said that he was a very emotional man. A couple of hours later he turned up at the party with a German woman and stood at the bar. I approached him. He found it uncomfortable and didn't want to look at me. I explained that I'd been up all night. I was very tired. I didn't like flying and just fell asleep. I also told him not to worry, I'll be leaving, but if you don't mind, could I stay for a few days holiday, seeing that I've made the effort to come out? He agreed to that before marching off with the German.

Can't say I was too displeased, but there was an immediate concern. I was almost out of cigarettes, and I had drunk most of the alcohol in Mick Jagger's second home. The village was a long way from the small town where all the shops were situated. I returned to my house and drank the last bottle of red wine and tried to make my remaining cigarettes last.

The following morning I got ready and went for a walk round the village trying to work out what to do. The only thing I could think of was to walk, but that was going to be an arduous journey, but I could see no other way until I saw a very tall woman with long hair, long legs, and a very short skirt about to get into her car. I asked if she would give me a lift into town. She agreed and off we went. She was French but we managed to converse in broken Spanish. When we pulled into town, I asked if she fancied a coffee before shopping. She agreed and as we walked into the bar I saw Mick Jagger sitting in there with a coffee and a whisky chaser. We sat down next to him. After a while, we started to talk, and so the atmosphere between us changed for the better. We had a few drinks and drove back to his house to have a few more. Then he opened up a box on the table that I instinctively knew contained dope. We had a few spliffs and a few drinks. As I was leaving he said, "Do you fancy a drive up to the Sierra Nevada tomorrow?"

"Yeah, that would be good," I replied.

I opened a bottle of wine that I'd bought from the supermercado and rolled a joint from the bit of dope that he had given me. The world was less stressful. I made my way up to the roof terrace and surveyed the dramatic scenery that I'd barely noticed until now. I was jobless, effectively homeless and alone, but I had a strengthening of my faith that things would turn out for the best.

The following day I made my way to his house. I was still unsure every time I knocked whether he would open the door or not, but he did. We got in his old Volvo estate and made our way up the very dangerous road that led out of the village. Our relationship was still very tentative; I didn't trust him, and he didn't trust me. We had that unreal dialogue you have with people you don't want to give anything away to. We began our ascent up the Sierra Nevada, stopping high up to fill his water bottles he had brought with him from the natural spring. It was icy cold, very crisp and very fresh. We returned to his car and continued the ascent. My stomach churned as we turned a corner. The sight was truly breathtaking. We were so high it was like being in a plane one minute after taking off. We carried on until we stopped for a drink in a town the other side of the Sierra Nevada. I was still so unsure of him that when I went to the toilet I had the strange feeling he might not be present when I returned, but he was. The next three days were spent drinking wine and smoking dope in his house and giving nothing away.

One morning when I was still in bed the doorbell sounded which was far too loud for the size of the house and irritated me greatly. I ignored it a few times before I heard Mick Jagger shouting: "Ray, Ray," through the door. I got up and pretended I had been napping on the roof terrace. Standing with Mick was a swarthy little fellah. Mick said that he was going to do the job, so we all trooped down to the basement. Mick Jagger was going to excavate some of the earth and turn it into another bedroom. They were speaking in Spanish. I wasn't really listening, I was just thinking: I hope they fuck off soon. Although I did catch the gypsy saying he was going to remove the earth with donkeys. As the gypsy was measuring and making notes, Mick Jagger turned to me and said, "He's got a massive dick."

"Sorry?"

"Yeah, he's fucked all the women in this village and the next two. They love him"

"I bet they do."

"You know that woman with the long legs that gave you a lift into town?"

"He's shagged her?"

"Yeah."

I finally got bored and decided to return home. I decided to get the coach as I was in no real hurry and had nothing in England to return to. Mick Jagger dropped me at the village to wait for the bus. There was no love lost in our farewell. I took the bus to Granada. From there I would get the bus to Madrid. It was late when I arrived in Granada. The next bus to Madrid was a good few hours away. There is nothing worse than being alone in a bus station at night knowing no one knows you are there.

When the time came to board the bus I'd drunk a few beers and was extremely tired.

As we pulled out of the bus station and made our way to the motorway, the last sight I saw was many prostitutes all lined up. The thing that struck me the most about them was that they all seemed to be exactly ten meters apart like a well-drilled military unit on parade. It was going to take a few hours to get to Madrid. I drifted away dreaming about prostitutes.

It was light when I woke again and there was still a way to go. I thought about staying in Madrid overnight. But by the time we arrived it just seemed too hectic. So I bought a ticket for a Barcelona bound bus which was leaving in an hour. I went to the toilet, threw some water on my face, and noticed how tired I looked. My legs were cramping and my arse was killing me. As we began to leave Madrid behind, I noticed a map with the bus's position on it, and Barcelona wasn't even on the map. That electronic map made the journey seem twice as long as I stared at it throughout the journey, willing it to move quicker. We stopped three times before the nothingness of the landscape began to steadily gain dwellings. As I stepped on Barcelona, I felt delirious. I needed a hotel. There was an information kiosk and I asked the woman in it for the nearest hotel. I booked in. Then I went to the shops to buy alcohol, cold meats and bread. I bought a bottle of wine and four lagers. I opened the wine and turned on the TV; oh, the luxury of being alone in a room with a bed. I decided that after a couple of glasses of wine I would go out and see a bit of the city. I woke and saw that the time was 12:30 am. I had bad cramp in my calves. I needed the rest, so I forwent the Barcelona night life. My next bus to Paris was not until 5:00 pm the following day. So I decided to stay in and make the most of the following day. I would get up early, and go and visit the Gaudi Cathedral. I've always liked architecture so I wasn't going to miss this opportunity to see it no matter how tired I felt. Apart from getting in and out of bed all night with debilitating cramp, I was up early and feeling good. I took a shower, packed and left my case with reception, then took the metro to the Sagrada Familia.

What a building!

Back on the bus, next stop Paris. It was early in the morning when we all trooped off at the Paris bus station. My next bus to London was in an hour. Then there was an announcement: The bus to London was going to be delayed by four hours. As those of us for the bus to London stood idly around shaking our heads in disappointment, I started to chat with an English guy who I'd recognized on the journey from Barcelona. Then we started to chat with a Romanian girl who had been robbed the night before in Paris. It was the first real conversation I had had since I started the grueling bus journey. There was nothing to do but go to a bar for a few hours. By the time I reached London I was exhausted. I made it to Charing Cross station from Kings Cross station by tube. As I emerged onto the concourse I was immediately confronted with the dark poetry that is commuting humanity. I stood there engulfed by the mass, trying to focus on the departures board for the next train to Tunbridge Wells.

I made two phone calls when I arrived home: One to C, saying I'll be collecting my books soon, and the other confirming I was up for the acid cleaning job. And so my world continued to turn.

A Bricklayer's Tales

Gary Troia

MRS. McCLINTOCK

Mrs. McClintock, of Glasgow, had closed the front door of her modest house for the very last time, but she was far too tearful to glance back when she reached the street. She got in the waiting taxi with her husband Robbie ,and drove the short distance to the local pub for their farewell party. Inside the pub were good luck banners and balloons that said, "Good Luck." The McClintocks had sold their modest home for a good profit and had bought a villa in the Andalusian countryside. The villa was in an urbanisation where mostly expats lived who had retired early to live the dream. The McClintocks dream was beginning to bear fruit and it was ripening in paradise. Every morning they took breakfast outside and admired the mountain views. Robbie cooked barbecues in the evening by the pool next to the lemon trees: Fresh sardines and juicy steaks with sumptuous salads; deep-fried was now just a distant memory from a very different way of life. The wine was cheap and Robbie soon took a liking for it. He only ever drank "heavy" and lager back in Scotland. Soon they were meeting their neighbours who invited the McClintocks to their barbecues, and the McClintocks would happily return the favour. The alcohol was so cheap and the barbecues so numerous that Robbie was in his element. Robbie used to think of his old friends in Glasgow. The only time they would ever venture out was to the pub on Friday night after work. Saturday after the football and Sunday before lunch; but here it was everyday - all day, if you fancied it. There didn't even have to be an excuse, just a sunny day full of nothing to do but invite people round for a bite to eat and a glass of wine by the pool, talking of home. Mrs. McClintock soon started to broaden her horizons. She became part of a group of women who arranged days out. One of their favourite trips was to take the bus to Malaga. They would tour the shopping district and have a bite to eat in a tapas bar. They became particularly excited when they found out that Primark was opening a store. "The Vino Tinto Girls," as they liked to call themselves, would each drink a glass of vino tinto on arrival at their destination. It had become a ritual. They were all dressed in their best on the day that Primark opened. After returning from each trip the Vino Tinto Girls would meet up with their husbands in a local bar.

The first year in paradise became the second year abroad.

Robbie was no longer waiting for lunch to have a glass of wine, he began drinking immediately after breakfast. Then it was with breakfast until he finally gave up the idea of breakfast all together. By the afternoon, he was so drunk that he would have to sleep it off. Mrs. McClintock would rouse him for his tea, which he pecked at like one of the little sparrows that hopped about on the patio, longing for the time when he could sit in his special chair berating characters on the TV with a bottle of wine at his side and a never empty glass in his hand. The McClintocks had rarely argued in Scotland – there was not too much to argue about. Robbie was a diligent worker who had always brought home the bacon, and both their daughters had turned out well. Now the arguments came thick and fast until one day they just stopped dead. No more arguing, no more talking: just silence. Robbie was perturbed that he could no longer drink at home in peace. Mrs. McClintock's silence was far too loud for that, so Robbie took to walking half a mile or so down the road to the local bar. It was there that he found kindred spirits with a ready-made drinking crew, about half a dozen or so on most days. Occasionally one or two others would join the group. At other times, there were one or two less, but the hardcore were always there. Robbie never missed a day; he could be relied upon. He was just that kind of man, hardly ever missing a day at work back in Glasgow.

One of the regular crew had an apartment above the bar. He held poker nights there. Not everyone played, but if you didn't play you could still drink. Some nights Robbie and the others would have to sleep on the settee and chairs as there was no way they could make it home. One night Robbie slept in a pullout bed with a woman called Maureen. Seedy groping took place throughout the night, which Robbie tried hard to forget in the morning. It was extremely hot and Robbie's head was pounding. The smell of the group's unwashed sweat in the room was pungent – Robbie would never forget that smell.

Mrs. McClintock began making regular trips back to Scotland on the pretext of visiting her daughters. Robbie was distraught and agreed to reign in his drinking and only going to the bar at weekends. For a time things did get better, but it was never quite the same between them. Mrs. McClintock used to enjoy sitting on the veranda at the front of their villa in the mornings. Deep in thought and more at peace with herself, she began to take in the sights and sounds of nature. She noticed insects that were quite different to those found in Britain. Huge flying beetles now caught her eye, a mixture of shimmering blacks and blues. What amazing colours she thought. Dear Little geckos crawled on her hand and settled. She also looked forward to the sweet sounding chimes from the bells around the goats' necks that jingled sweetly as they were lead from the bottom of the hill, soon to be passing by her villa. As the goats began to pass, the goat herder would always drop his staff out of respect and acknowledgement of Mrs. McClintock as he pressed on with his herd. Mrs. McClintock would give a little wave in return.

Robbie would usually emerge from the villa looking a little sheepish, and say: "just off for a couple of pints down the bar, love." Mrs. McClintock would nod and reply, "enjoy," before getting lost again in her new found reverence for nature." She began to buy books on local wildlife, becoming quite adept at naming the different insects that she saw. She even bought a little journal and attempted to recreate the insects with a pencil. Once she had drawn a certain insect, she would write the name of the species below it.

The chimes of the goats' bells seemed herald a call to prayer for Mrs. McClintock; and she did pray in her own little way. She also began to feel herself becoming a little too eager to see the goat herder. One morning she decided to ask his name. She knew how to say hello and how are you? In Spanish, so thought she would give it a go. As the little goat herder neared her villa she said hola. He smiled back mostly with his eyes as he kept moving along with his herd.

Mrs. McClintock bought a Spanish learning pack and each day learnt more Spanish. She became quite proficient to the point where she paid a local woman to speak with her once a week. As she grew more confident she opened up a dialogue with the little goat herder. Soon he was stopping for a glass of cooling water. Pepito lived in an old farmhouse without running water or electric and washed himself in the local river. Mrs. McClintock just could not comprehend the amount of hours he spent with the goats. She also admired the fact that Pepito had never once complained about his laborious life. On the contrary, Pepito began to expound on the far-reaching freedom he had.

When Mrs. McClintock felt low, when the

grilles on her windows really stood for bars on a prison cell, Mrs. McClintock thought of Pepito's large smiling eyes that shone with peace, and soon she began to break out of herself.

Robbie soon forgot his weekend only pledge, returning from the bar every day drunk. He had lost so much weight with the continual drinking and lack of food. Nevertheless, Mrs. McClintock had never felt freer or so serene and continued to look forward to the tinkling of the goat bells that proclaimed the imminent arrival of Pepito. One day, in winter, Mrs. McClintock thought of Pepito having to wash in the cold river. She had a crazy idea - an absurd idea. When she saw him later, she would insist on him having a bath in the villa.

After that thought, Mrs. McClintock could hardly contain herself. She went dashing around the villa like an infatuated teenage girl. Her heart was pounding when she heard the first bells start to chime. By the time Pepito had reached the McClintocks villa, and more than ready for his customary drink and sandwich, Mrs. McClintock thought she was going to faint. As she handed him his cup of tea, she blurted out, "Fancy a bath?" Turning a deep crimson by the time the last word left her mouth.

Pepito just smiled and took her up on the offer as if he was accepting one of her cheese and pickle sandwiches. She ran the bath and put two clean towels out for him. She then went to the kitchen to make lunch for them both. After making the sandwiches, she walked to the lounge to wait for him, but noticed that the bathroom door was wide open. He saw her and smiled serenely.

"Do you want me to scrub your back," she said calmly. His smile answered that question. Within the next few seconds Mrs. McClintock was scrubbing the tanned back of the little goat herder and humming a tune she could not put a name to.

Neither Mrs. McClintock nor the goat herder heard the drunken Robbie stagger through the front door.

"What the fucking hell is going on here?" screamed Robbie.

"Oh, I'm just scrubbing the goat herders back," replied Mrs. McClintock. "He doesn't have running water at home."

The goat herder turned his head and smiled serenely at Robbie. Robbie attempted to fly into a rage but staggered instead, falling to the floor in a drunken heap. He managed to pick himself up. He saw one of his golf clubs in a large umbrella stand. He grabbed it and turned to the bathroom where he saw a naked goat herder standing in his bath. The goat herder was still smiling. He had his crook in his hands. For the first time in a long time, maybe ever, Robbie heard a voice from within that told him it was all over. His shoulders slumped. He let go of the golf club and went sobbing to the bedroom where he lay down and fell asleep.

After finishing his bath, Pepito told Mrs. McClintock to pack some things for the night, as she would be coming to stay at his farmhouse. She wasted no time in packing a case. Within in twenty minutes or so, Mrs. McClintock and the goat herder were both leading the herd of goats home.

The second year abroad became the third year in paradise.

Mrs. McClintock wakes very early these days to wave the goat herder goodbye. She waves until he is out of sight, then settles down in an old rocking chair drawing insects in her journal, waiting for Pepito's smiling eyes to return.

A Bricklayer's Tales

Gary Troia

THE UNCHANGEABLE CHAMELEON

What are my earliest memories?
Funnily enough, my earliest memories happen to be my most vivid and enduring memories of my life. I can remember watching blokes cleaning their cars on a Sunday and I used to think how boring, can't you think of anything else to do? I mean, it almost gets me raging now. I also remember my dad taking me to the house of his fancy woman. He thought I was too young to know what was going on, but I wasn't. I can recall that image clearer than what I had for breakfast this morning.
School?
I have fewer memories of school than any other period in my life. I used to go to

primary school and pretend I could speak foreign languages. I say foreign languages, mainly French really, as I found I could manipulate the sounds easier than Spanish or German. Secondary school begets fewer memories than any other period in my life. The only memorable moment was when some students burned it down.

Was I involved?

No, but I knew those who did it, and I witnessed them doing it.

My most profound memory was also the worst moment I ever had in school. I remember going to a meeting for all the kids who were staying on for the following sixth form. I actually went to the meeting knowing it was all over for me. I sat through that meeting knowing an apprenticeship in Bricklaying was my immediate destiny as my jealousy towards the studious kids and their further two years of study was, perhaps, the commencement of a resentment that led to an unshakable lifetime of deep-rooted depression and anger.

I've spent my whole life trying to get away from construction and brickwork – not that there is anything wrong with the game – it's just the worst job in the world for me. Even when I moved to the states, I ended up laying brick and block.

After deportation from the states for bringing in a small quantity of hash, I studied hard and got a degree. That degree helped me to get a job teaching brickwork in a college.

The bus-driving incident?

It was do or die, anything other than brickwork. I saw an advert for a bus-driving job in my local garage and got it. I hated that too. Especially the early morning shifts. The yellow-orange fluorescent lights of the garage, the public, and, of course, the inspector who had it in for me from the moment we met. He was on my back continuously. Everything was a problem. It went on and on for months. I only had to see his face and the hairs on the back of my neck stood up like a hunting dog; think I used to growl, too. Then one day as I was bringing in the 47B to the depot, a single-decker, ten minutes late, there he was, his large condescending face giving me the look that said, I've been trying to get you out, and I will be always trying to get you out. I just flipped. I put my foot on the accelerator and rammed the 47B hard into him. I saw his proud head smash into the windscreen with incredible force. It split in parts like a watermelon thrown to the floor. He died instantly, apparently.

Do I regret it? Can't say I do.

"How are you going to contend with your time in here?"

Write some nonsense.

"Fiction?"

No, I'm determined.

A Bricklayer's Tales

Gary Troia

A BRICKLAYER'S TALE

It is set for five-fifteen, but it never goes off. No matter how much I've had to drink the night before, I always wake before the bloody thing has the chance. I read in a book one time that said if you visualize a clock set at the time you want to get up, then you do. I spend the extra time gained thinking about the things that have gone wrong in my life, the terrible decisions I've made, people that have loved and left me, my work. This is the big problem. I'm always in the past, racked by guilt, or worrying about the future.

At work, I'm known as "Posh Ray." It's an absolute joke. I'm a bricklayer, fer fuck's sake. The reason I got called Posh Ray was that sometimes I would read The Times or The Guardian in the canteen. I got comments like: "Ray, who d'ya think you are, posh or sumfink? Ha, ha, ha. "Av" yer shares gone up? Ha, ha, ha." According to their reasoning I should have been reading The Sun, The Daily Sport, or The Mirror at a push.

Anyway, it don't matter, the name stuck. I live in a rented room. It's terribly depressing - but at least it's Friday. I'll probably spend the weekend drinking wine and smoking joints. My whole life encased in a 10 x 8 room. It's my birthday Sunday: sixty–fucking-two! My stomach flips at the thought of this, like the feeling in a nightmare when you're falling. I don't know how this has happened to me with nothing to show for that amount of time. To be fair, I do know. I'm a liar. I'm an alcoholic.

Even when I was on the up for a while I knew it would never last because I could never cope with reality. The voice would soon start calling: "time to self-medicate, Ray." Then the drinking would start.

One time, the worst time, I drank myself out of a good job and a promising relationship into a bedsit without any furniture. It was a bedsit in the truest sense of the word. I cannot put into words how frightened I was then. I felt my soul had left me. It wasn't till much later I realised that it was I who had moved far away from it.

I look at my face in the mirror and assure myself it doesn't look as bad as most my age; but it's old nevertheless. I spit into the sink and watch the blood from my gum disease, mingled with toothpaste, swirling down the plughole. It's really cold and the radiators don't come on till 8:00 am. I'll be at work and working for half an hour before they even kick in.

If I'd some money, not a lot, just enough to live frugally for a month, to pay my rent, to buy my drugs: Oh what joy that would be. But I don't, and it's nearly Christmas. That means two weeks off without pay, so it's important that I don't lose a day.

I'm working on a large refurbishment job. It's by the river, so it's even colder there. Fuck it! I am short on t–shirts. I'm going to have to rummage around the laundry basket and sniff out the least offensive. When I say laundry basket, I mean the pile of shite on the floor that represents my laundry basket. I look at this festering pile and assume that the top two are the best bet. I tentatively sniff them hoping for a result. It's not pleasant, but I slip both of them on anyhow, focusing the antiperspirant mainly at the pits. I've not been to the laundry for weeks, and I'm not sure whether Margaret (the seventy–two year old woman who owns the house) is ever going to get round to having the washing machine fixed. I splash my face with water (what my Gran would have called a cat's lick) and have a piss. I pull on my work jeans, which have a horrid feel to them: lifeless and embedded with mortar from the past couple of weeks. The right hand pocket is hanging off my anorak. Then me old boots. This is a bit of an effort. The blood rushes to my head as I bend to put them on. The right one has a hole in it that lets in puddles. I drag my hand across my face with a tired sigh, it is the first time I have encountered the headache today. I spy with my little eye my weekly travel-pass that sits by the side of my portable TV on the shabby yellow Formica table. I've forgotten that before.

Also on the table are some remnants of the night before: wine bottle, ashtray, tumbler and multi–vitamins. Two other wine bottles are on the floor. One is definitely dead, but the other is only wounded still offering a good glassful. The ashtray is overflowing, yet I am overjoyed to see yet another brother-in-arms, a joint with at least two good lugs left in him. The thought of drinking and smoking brings immediate watery bile to my mouth. It keeps on coming. I keep on swallowing. Soon enough the uprising of bile begins to relent. Finally, I can swallow alcohol and smoke. I heave continuously as I descend the uncarpeted stairs where only the grippers remain.

I open the door. Jesus, I think, as an icy blast hits me hard. I walk to the station wondering how much of a future remains to me, but get distracted by a crisp packet whipped up by the wind - always with the fucking entropy.

I queue for coffee at the station but remove myself from the line when I realize I'm sixpence short of a cup. I envy those with coffee and tea.

Everyone tries to avoid the seat next to me as they quite rightly don't want to get brick dust on them. Ultimately, someone will sit there as no one wants to stand for over half an hour to London.

I forgot to mention that when I got home yesterday there was a letter waiting for me. Margaret had placed it on the uncarpeted fourth step as she always does with my mail. I've been receiving a lot of mail recently, mostly from my doctor and the hospital. I can't deal with opening them. I pick them up from the fourth stair and place them in a pile behind the portable TV. Before I left this morning I placed yesterday's letter in the inside pocket of my anorak. I'm not sure when I will read it, but it will have to be the right time and place as I'm very superstitious when it comes to opening letters.

We're pulling into London Bridge. The train empties around a third of the passengers and more than a third of the train-tension. Waterloo is the penultimate. Charing Cross is the ultimate and mine.

I get a cup of coffee from McDonalds, which is bitter and cheap, but means I've enough money left over for a tea at work. The station clock says that I have time to nip outside and drink it along with one or two cigarettes before I descend the stairs to the district line. I think of the letter. I think of my age. I think of the past. I think what could have been if I'd thought differently. The tube-train rattles on. I think about where I'm working: a huge old office block that the bank of ABC is renovating. I think of the foreman who calls himself the Viking. He is known by this moniker throughout the London construction world. He is an absolute fanny, nothing like a Viking - at least nothing like how I imagine a Viking. He's even written Viking on his hard hat with a magic marker. I think of my bag of tools, the tools of my trade. Rusty tools. I never clean my trowel properly at the end of the working day. I just slam it sideways into the spot board two or three times to get rid of most of the muck (mortar). I like to get away from the site as soon as possible. I don't have time for cleaning tools. I go rushing into the street, but when I get there I realise I don't really have anywhere to go, or anyone to see. So I go to the pub instead and think about it all some more.

Tower Hill is where I get off. I think of where I'm working again, and how cold it will be on the sixth floor river side. Walking over Tower Bridge is unpleasant. I can't remember it being colder this year, but I could be wrong. I protect one hand in my left anorak pocket, the other rests on the torn seam taking the full brunt of winter. A clock on one of the buildings I'm walking towards tells me I have time for a cuppa before I start. A pleasant thing. I hold the tea tightly with my cold hand. I sit at one of the long benches in the canteen. I close my eyes as the world starts to spin. I can't face the thought of talking to anyone, so I take my tea to the sixth floor. I place it by a concrete column and fetch my tools from under a sheet of insulation where I hid them yesterday.

I lean on a horizontal scaffold tube that stops the workers from falling off the building. I look at boats on the Thames bobbing around. I imagine myself on one of them. I even imagine looking at myself from the boat at me leaning on the scaffold tube looking back at me on the boat. The muck is already on my spot board. The laborers get in half an hour before the brickies to ensure there will be no hanging about. My cheeks are stinging from the steely wind. I take the trowel out of my bag and scrape the remaining muck off that wasn't expelled when I hit it on the board yesterday. I'm already four courses up, which is good as the blood would rush to my head if I had to start from the concrete. I start three minutes early. This is not to impress anyone, as I've never tried to impress anyone ever at work. I've been sacked many times, not because I'm no good, just that I'm indifferent to it all. I can't be indifferent for the next couple of weeks as I need the money to get through the unpaid holiday.

I hear the Viking walking up the stairs talking to the others in his pseudo hard-man way. I anticipate what is coming. He emerges onto the floor I'm working on and shouts out in mock humor, whilst holding his stomach with one hand and tapping his watch with the other: "Look out! Ray's only working. Dave, Dave," he shouts below, "Ray's only fucking working and it's not even 'alf – past," still tapping his watch.

I ignore him. When he is far enough away, I close my eyes, reach within and embrace my soul in atonement. I sense it withdraw to the boat I am looking at. Telepathically I send out "goodbye"... and telepathically I receive "goodbye."

Every time I bend to take the muck from the board, my head begins to pound and the pain increases. I roll the mortar on the board, working it around the whole of the pier I'm building. I take a brick from the stack and ease it gently down. The excess muck, which squeezes out, is scraped off to be used for the perp joint on the next brick. This procedure is repeated continuously until the working day is done.

I assume an hour must have passed, but it hasn't, the clock on an adjacent building tells me thirty-two minutes have. I decide to do another ten minutes and then go to the toilet. I don't want to use the toilet - I just need to sit down. Apart from two half–hour breaks in the nine hour day, the only place to have a rest is in the toilet. As this is a big job, they have installed proper toilets, not quite as good as public toilets, but better than the plastic little crapper we had on the last job that stank to high heaven; I rested less there.

Ten minutes or so later I am in the rest area. On returning to my workstation, I remember the letter. So I decide to lay another three courses, joint them up and go for a little read.

As I descend the stairs, I hear a commotion going on. I look round the corner of the stair well and see the Viking with his trusted lieutenants. Dave the head-hoddy, and Bret the charge—hand. As I stand and look at them, everything so loud and monotonous, I wonder what really goes through their minds? Is it always just the banal, or are they just too afraid to reveal their true selves to each other?

By the Viking's table, there is a hoist, which brings the materials. I shake my head in disbelief that they will remain the same throughout their lives, laughing and joking, scrambling around building sites, not being miserable like me with my superior awareness.

I walk to the toilets and search for one that reeks least and has no leftovers. I rummage in my anorak pocket for the letter. I feel the letter. I also feel something suspiciously like a joint—butt. It is. What a find. It's skunk, too. I light it. I inhale…I exhale. The smell of grass begins to pervade the toilets. I'm feeling better already. I take another toke and open the letter. It is strange but I feel this letter holds my whole life within it. I read it and place it back in my pocket. I smile to myself, a proper smile, one that has true depth. Should I tell someone about it, but there is no one to tell. I've a sister in Canada, but we lost touch some time ago. I only really have drinking and drugging associates. I take the last toke and close my eyes. The letter is from my Doctor and says that I have been diagnosed with inoperable, stage four pancreatic cancer, and why haven't I been in touch, and I should be getting in touch right away without further delay.

When I open my eyes, everything seems more pronounced and clearer than usual. The toilet roll holder without toilet paper seems interesting. Now I'm laughing at inane graffiti: "had a great big curry, now I do a poo, the brown stuffs down the toilet, I leave the smell for you." I stand up, open the door, go to the plastic mirrors, and see a reflection there that has boundless freedom and joy within it. Whatever I felt previously about my life, there now seems to be an ultimate meaning to it. So much weight removed.

I leave the toilets and walk to the floor where the Viking has his table. I see the Viking standing close behind Dave and doing a doggy-style movement with everyone standing around laughing. Without a thought to what I'm doing, I start jogging towards them. I'm picking up speed now and laughing to myself like "Dick Dastardly's" dog "Muttley." Dave was the first to notice. He turned his head whilst still being shagged from behind. The Viking stopped his pretend shagging and looked too. They seem to be standing in awe, as the running man, without a soul, just the husk of a body functioning solely on memory, gains on them quickly.

There is a gap between the scaffolding and the hoist. I focus on the gap before realizing that I am now airborne. I manage with consummate ease, like an Olympic gymnast, a 180-degree turn and see the faces of Dave, Bret and the Viking, with their mouths open, aghast, while mine is smiling. I feel like I am standing on a plinth of air, suspended for what seems like an inordinate amount of time until, imperceptibly at first, I begin the descent. To me it feels I'm going the way of the twin towers, not over and twisting, but straight down, feet first, in perfect alignment, finally free.

From the boat, I witness the body falling from the building site. I notice too, a letter fluttering above it. I watched it fall gently into the Thames; now we are both finally free.

****

A Bricklayer's Tales

ABOUT THE AUTHOR

Gary Troia was born in southeast London and studied Spanish and Philosophy at Middlesex University and the Universidad de Deusto.

In 2010, he left behind a career in education and moved to a small Spanish village, where he began his lifelong dream of writing.

His first book, Spanish Yarns and Beyond, is a humorous account of his time in Spain. 'A great play on words, witty and well written,' was how one reviewer described the book.

A Bricklayer's Tales, published in 2013, is a collection of ten tales, including: Angel Dust, the peculiar story of a man whose new life in America leads to conversations with Ancient Greek philosophers. Mrs. McClintock, an absurd farce in which a Glaswegian couple retire to Spain, and A Bricklayer's Tale, the story of a disillusioned, alcoholic bricklayer.

Since then Gary has gone on to write seven books.

Gary now lives in Hampshire, with his partner Marina where he continues to write.

A NOTE FROM THE AUTHOR

Thank you for reading my book.
If you enjoyed the book and If you ever have a spare moment, it would be a great help if you could post a review of it and let other potential readers know why you liked it. It's not necessary to write a lengthy formal review—a summary would be great.

SAMPLE FROM:

RAY DENNIS DOES *THE SECRET*

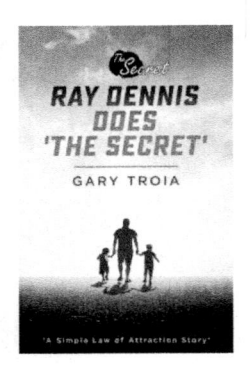

CHAPTER ONE

I'd gone west and created a new life. I was living in an apartment complex in Manassas, Virginia that had a swimming pool and a small gym: Completely unthinkable and undoable on a bricklayer's wage in England. But now I am back in England in my old childhood bedroom with a threadbare carpet, dry plaster audibly crumbling from the walls behind the western scene wallpaper, and an ill-fitting sash window causing the room to be freezing. The weather would be balmy in LA right now. I looked at my passport and stared at the latest stamp that was over my American visa. It said "Undesirable Alien". I do not usually drink spirits, but that night only whisky was gonna see me through. I gulped it down quickly to prevent loss, sadness and stupidity from overwhelming me. My hands were shaking like an old drunk in the streets, and the glass rattled between my teeth. A quarter of the bottle allowed my mind respite for an answer to emerge that might miraculously get me back to where I recently was; but every madcap idea was destroyed by the image of undesirable alien stamped indelibly on my visa, my heart, and mind.

"Do you want something to eat, love?" my Nan called from downstairs.
"No thanks, Nan," I replied from the

landing. "I'm really tired after the flight, so I'm just sleeping tonight. Thanks anyway."

"Well, there is some corned beef if you fancy a sandwich a bit later."

"Okay, thanks."

I heard her shut the living room door. After a time I was slightly more comfortable within myself. It was a paradoxical uncomfortable comfort, but it was the best that I was gonna achieve that night. Then I felt the tough winter air duck in through the loose-fitting sash window and jab me with icy punches that I was no match for. I crawled between the sheets and curled up in the fetal position, taking frequent swigs from my bedside medicine. I was so cold and so lonely that I needed to be drunk and oblivious, as I know all too well that tomorrow and the near future will be much, much worse than the shock of being deported from my recent life in America. I turned in bed and through the ill-fitting sash window I glimpsed the large red neon cross on the local church that seemed to offer me a refuge and a hell simultaneously.

The last thing I wanted was for morning to come. I've never liked mornings. Mornings reminded me of getting up as a bricklayer and traveling to the other side of London to lay bricks on yet another miserable building site under always grey clouds. I used to have a big brass alarm clock. The constant ticking of each second was so loud it kept me awake all night long in a constant state of panic. I would have loved the timeframe of a three month night (at least) to sort myself out. No human contact. No responsibility. No talking. No job. No nothing. Then, through my despicable despair, a sensible thought managed to wriggle its way to the forefront of my mind. It told me that the money sitting in my American bank account might be frozen or stolen by the American authorities, so I decided to withdraw as much as I could the following day, and that will be my task until

I had removed it all. Then I will not have to bother or worry about looking for work, for a while.

Gradually my old friends who heard through the grapevine that I was back in town, phoned to get the news of why I was back in town. I agreed to meet them when I was on the phone, but as the time drew near for them to arrive, I left the house and walked the short distance to the beginning of the woods, where I sat on a bench and waited long enough for them to leave. The phone calls stopped. I alternated between the local off-licences where I bought my whisky and wine as I did not want to appear an alcoholic. I also prescribed myself an assortment of drugs as whisky and wine were not nearly enough.

Spring is the great womb of life, and for me, as an April child, it seemed doubly so. I was aware and relieved that my desperate despair was dissipating. I began to take long walks through the woods where the density of life was almost palpable. I knew a way through the woods that led to a plateau, and it was there with the spring sun on my face where I began to contemplate why my ups were followed by such severe downs. The very thought of whisky turned my stomach, and a perceived joint weakened me immediately to the point of mild paranoia. The healing and recovery process had begun, but this time I had to find a higher ground where the highs are higher and the lows are not so low. A new way of being had to be found that was going to enable this leopard to change its spots.

So the question was: How do I go about changing them? First, I was thinking that I needed to conquer the past. I knew that my father must shoulder some of the blame of why I was like I was. He was never interested, beat me around, not violently, mildly, but it certainly left an impression on my character. He was a compulsive gambler who nearly lost our house, and the deeds of my Nan's house too, after he had used it as collateral in a failed attempt at being a greengrocer. After that he did the only thing that he could conceive of doing - running away, which left my Mum having to do two jobs so we would not all be homeless. This was my first eureka moment that gave me some insight as to why I was the way I was. I had subconsciously and naturally taken on some of the traits that my father had by osmosis. My mind whirred with consequent thoughts, but I had to stop myself as I didn't want to uncover more knowledge and end up forgetting it as I had no pen and paper to document my findings. I went immediately to W.H. Smith and bought a diary, pens, pencils, notepad and some brightly coloured felt-tip pens. On returning home with my items, I wrote down I had unwittingly taken on many traits and characteristics from my father, but as I waited for the next revelation to be revealed, my mind had gone silent on the issue. I wondered why I drank too much. My father did not drink at all, and this threw my thesis into doubt. I had never done anything of note at school. Never done any homework. Never passed an exam, and was urged into an apprenticeship in brickwork - a job that was such an uneasy fit for me that I felt I had been sentenced to a working life full of hard labour. I remember being in the same room as all the children that were staying on to do their A Levels and then on to bright futures. I honestly believe that there was some kind of voice that had led me to that room to make me always remember how I had fucked up good and proper. I was the only child in that room who was not staying on. It is true that bricklaying enabled me to work in America, but from being in a great position there, I had ruined that by getting up to no good.

I was unable to get to the bottom of exactly

why I was the way I was, and had never had any true and worthwhile guidance from anyone in my life on how to be. No discipline. No goals, although I always had a good roof over my head, nourishing food and decent clothes. The answer to my problems, and the way out of it seemed always to be hanging in the air somewhere close by, but it was ephemeral and I could neither grasp it or comprehend it, but I sensed for sure that there was a definite answer. I grew frustrated and turned again to my two best friends, drink and drugs. They helped me to stop thinking about anything much at all.

Printed in Great Britain
by Amazon